Life After

A Memoir of Inspiration Post Survival

Written by Tamecka-Grate Frazier

ISBN-13: 978-0-578-72422-5

Publisher's Note

Dedication

I dedicate this book to my Omnipotent Lord and Savior, Jesus Christ, to the courageous people who have told their stories. To those who have paved the way, and to those who have yet to share.

We all have a story to tell. Therefore I dedicate this book to YOU!

Contents

"There's no set time for healing from trauma, there's no anecdote that speeds up the process, be patient with you and allow yourself to live. Once you start to live, it's then you'll start to heal"

Tamecka Grate-Frazier

Introduction

May 2020,

In the memoir, "Life After," – I'll escort you down a path that shares my real narrative for survival, triumph, and perseverance post a very traumatic experience. But before I do, I'll give you the prelims of what I remember most before this in-depth journey really began. Growing up in the Southeast part of Dallas, Texas, and born the only girl to my parents, raised with three brothers, I had no choice but to be feisty and outspoken, with an immeasurable amount of character. My earlier childhood days were topped off with tomboyish, go-getter poise. If my brothers could do it, so could I. I wanted to play football, softball, dodge ball, and any other kind of ball. Running "hood" track was my strength and favorite. My brothers told me as long as I had my shoes off, I was the fastest on our street and would represent Rust College Dr well. Preparing for our neighborhood track meets were the most fun.

I'd even get in on the building of bike ramps and makeshift basketball goals, and many scars later, I was considered a pretty TOUGH and bossy girl, and a true daddy's girl. As a daddy's girl, I'd find myself taken back by him daily, as he would make sure I knew I was his little queen instead. Very organized and tidy, my mom always carried herself in a "ladylike" manner, so my peripheral reach for my girlie instincts wasn't far off. I'd later find that sports were not for me, spending more time channeling my feminine abilities by finding a love for backyard singing and dancing with my childhood girlfriends. We even had our group. We'd dress up, host events, and bake mud pies and cook "grass" green beans. Our dolls became our audience, children, and students, as we would feed them the delights from our outdoorsy menu. Through the years, I'd have my share of occasional fistfights and downfalls like all kids in our era, who'd break up and make up within the hour. Extrovert and witty were my strongest character traits, traits that would later build me a Rolodex full of friendships. I never met a stranger. My classroom experiences were full of days of laughter with a hint of discipline, where I'd get reprimanded often for having high ranks in sco'ing, now considered harmless roasting. I'd later take this same energy and find my love for cheerleading.

Always seen, always heard. I had the opportunity to spend countless days and nights with my cousins, who were more like siblings. I had the best and firmest grandparents ever. My earlier life was full of ups and very few downs. Our upbringing was closer to that of the middle-class sector and afforded me a lifestyle of structure and comfort. My parents worked hard to provide a life of consistency. We took family trips, went to dinner once a week, and countless picnics and outings at the lake. These fond memories were my foundation. I was embraced with love and compassion. I had a family full of protection. My grandmothers were rooted in church and made sure we were too; Jesus was always at my reach. And although my adolescent years would bring a few unexpected shifts, with the breakup of my parents, I still felt a sense of protection. Almost to a fault that fostered vulnerability, that would later cause me to make some unconscious decisions for acceptance and social awareness.

By then, I'd faced what I considered turmoil that the average adult woman wouldn't be able to bear. Although there was no physical or mental presence of trauma that stemmed from any of these instances, I didn't realize that life's challenges would later present themselves to erase that blanket of protection that I relied so heavily upon.

Having conquered this in segments, I would unknowingly be building strength for an attack on my life that was deemed one of the most astounding medical miracles ever documented. An attack that would further propel my faith and existence into media streams across the globe, affording me a platform of a lifetime to later share a message that would touch anyone who'd experienced a life-changing event.

It's was even determined by surgeons, at one of our country's most sought trauma hospitals, that without God's grace, I could never repeat the feat. Having survived the ordeal that stemmed from domestic violence, "spillage" was still mind-boggling. How a friendly hello and the comfort of sharing a phone could turn so deadly who knows. A mere victim of circumstance. This opened up the doors of the unimaginable acceptance of having an actual brush with death, primarily having known that it could have happened to anyone. However, I was "chosen" by faith, the faith that drives the stamina needed to become an advocate. I was chosen to share my factual stories of endurance with multitudes of people. And I was expected to do it with the anticipation of conveying a message of hope with others who have also had similar accounts of trauma or if nothing less as a means of being a preventative measure. I was charged with making all well aware of how your life can change within a matter of minutes, fourteen to be exact.

I attribute my reason for my will to live to my faith, my foundational strength, and the support of uncountable family and friends. My message is to convey that even as traumatic of an experience it was, I was given another opportunity at life. My purpose is to share with others the steps and measures that I took and still do take to show it can be done. "Life After" has increased my self-love, confidence, courage, and overall will to live purposely. Living my "best" life is the goal, and the core of that goal includes helping others do the same. There is "Life After" is the footprint that I want to leave. It doesn't stop at the trial or place of pain.

If you believe your life has any meaning, you can overcome anything. My purpose is still prevalent, and even though it almost been 25 years and resonates just like yesterday, I know that it is my duty to God and society never to let my testimony lie dormant and show you what "Life After" looks like.

So, as you take this journey with me, please know that my sole intent is designed to embrace your heart and the hearts of others who may have experienced anything that may have left you lost and hopeless. To inspire the overcomer who has yet to share. And to catapult you into an awareness of restoration and empowerment. To pique the interest of the believer and encourage the non-believer to grasp ahold of God's unwavering faith, knowing that your life has a purpose and there are great rewards when you acknowledge and begin to fulfill it.

Chapter 1

The Foundation of Strength

I t was 1976, an era in time that allowed most
children to play outside without distraction, and
with the comfort of being able to trust your
neighbors, without second-guessing. I was five
years old, doing what most five-year-old little girls
do. My brothers, who were a few years older, were
playing with their friends, further away in the
distance, and both parents were inside of our home,
tending to house duties, but within arm's reach.
Although I was playing outside alone, or with
Pennie, Pennie was my imaginary friend, I was
always sanctioned to the front yard only, not to
come close to the sidewalk. This was a time where
what was understood, did not need repeating. So, in
the front yard, I played, and in the front yard, I
stayed.

At the break of dawn, the streets lights would
soon be on, and it would be time to close out a full
day of hopscotch, jacks, and mud pies. However, on
this day, I remember standing there, watching other
kids say their "goodbyes" while walking to their

homes, as the same rules applied in every household. I looked up to see my brothers running up the street, full speed ahead, racing to see who could outrun the other to the front door. They both were laughing and giggling, not recognizing that I was there, as I continued to stand still in the front yard. I could hear my mom saying, "Slow down! Where's Tamecka?" Suddenly, I felt a hard push from behind, and as quickly as it happened, I landed face down on the ground.

He fell atop of me and began gyrating his private parts upon my body as he grabbed my inner thigh and panties with his hand. Having had the wind knocked out of me from the fall, I was unable to see right away who it was and within a matter of seconds it was over, I then saw a very familiar boy running swiftly up the street. As I lay there crying, my mom, who was already calling for me, hysterically ran over to me, asking me what was wrong and immediately called for my dad. I slightly remember telling them that a boy had pushed me down and touched me there, pointing to my genital area, and without a thought, my parents called the police, and the police summoned an ambulance, which would then take me to the hospital to be examined.

To think, I was a five-year-old and able to give out vivid details of what happened. The visit to the doctor and the police engagement were all a blur; the final thing I recall from that night is my mom crying tears of happiness because the test showed that there was no penetration. No penetration, but a violation. Violation of everything that she and my dad would try to protect me from.

As I sit back and think on this time, I'm often reminded that it was not that day 1976 when the vividness or understanding of what occurred surfaced in my life, it wasn't until years later when I had conquered some of life's most challenging situations that I was reminded. I know it was blocked out of my mind for that very reason, and this has allowed me to face what's to come ahead without feeling victimized.

"Girl he likes you," my fellow cheerleader friend shared, I said "who?" and she replied, "that guy over there," as she pointed.

This is a phrase I never knew would follow me years later.

I was young and thriving and enjoying my early high school moments. It was the beginning of my sophomore school year. I was a member of the Junior Varsity cheerleading squad, we were preparing to take a bus to a football game against one of our rivalry schools, and this was the news that was delivered right before we left the school for the game. I was already hyped, and this revelation just put me on 10.

I was beyond giddy and did my best not to let it show, but not for long. What 16-year-old girl wouldn't be excited about a boy liking her, especially one that was very popular? In an instant, I'd already put our names in lights. Not knowing that those lights would later dim out quicker than a doused fire. And although the dimming came without notice, it would take me years to rid myself of the embarrassing stigma. You see what I had mistaken for love, turned into fascination, and that within two years, would lead to abuse. Never would I think there'd be a correlation. I couldn't believe that someone who claimed to "Like" and later "Love" me would bring harm to me in any way. I couldn't have been more from right.

The strength of making someone else more comfortable with themselves and their actions without regard to yourself or your own is a form of abuse. Throughout this entire relationship, I'd spend a great deal of time trying to convince him that our connection was secure, and he'd never need to feel the sense of insecurity that wreaked in his presence every day. This only fueled the situation, and as long as there was ever a question mark, it would inevitably be coupled with an unwarranted bout with abuse.

With one offensive occasion after another, I find myself covered in grace, with an impossible will to move on. This ultimately led to a boost of esteem that fostered my own need to love myself and build from the confidence I always knew I had. It didn't stop because of death or an attempt thereof. It didn't cease because of law enforcement. It ended because I finally took a stand concerning my life and demanded it to. I knew my worth was more than any level of someone else's insecurities. Finding myself free of this famine, with my head held high, I just knew I was ready to take on life. Or at least I thought. Consequently, our paths did not end with constraint, we'd soon reconcile it into a friendship of support, support that I never knew would be needed in the years to come.

I had since been privileged with the task of motherhood. The mother of a little boy, one that I prayed would never be stricken with the diabolical forces of the situations previously mentioned. What lay ahead would only bring about a list of questions.

However, the one question that was never posed was, "Why me," because of my strength, it was, "Why not me?" Well, let's just see…

A Miracle

1995, a year where Domestic Terrorism made a considerable mark, with the bombing of the Federal Building in downtown Oklahoma. Michael Jordan returned to the NBA, and OJ Simpson was found innocent. News that was noteworthy enough for me to continue the discussion for many years ahead.

That was until New Year's Eve, a time when thankfulness and culmination of one year and the transition into what usually is change, new goals, desires, and new beginnings of another.

December 31, 1995, usually started as it would, being a single mother, I woke my son, who was four years old at the time and fed him breakfast. We started our day by going to visit friends and family. After a full day of hanging out, we proceeded to my mother's house, where I knew my son would be staying for the rest of the evening. After my plans to see my then-boyfriend would change, my cousin and I decided to have a girl's evening out to bring in the New Year, overriding the decision to bring it in at church. She and I would hang out often, and I knew we were sure to have a great time.

After a night of fun, the typical protocol would be to stay the night with one another, as a safety precaution, any time we had gone out.

Instead, I headed home alone, in the wee hours of the night, ready for some quiet time and a chance to cook a New Year's Day meal the next day. During the ride home, there was a moment of concern, and the worry stemmed from hoping not to run into a drunk driver, who was out just as late as I was, or the misfiring of a shotgun, which was celebratory and typical of bringing in the new year. My drive home was successful. Being a single mother and living in a broad set of apartments, was always a reason to be cautious of my surroundings, and tonight was no different. As I approached my apartment complex of 30 something buildings up to 16 units each, I see a neighbor standing directly outside of the building in which I lived. After I parked the car, I sat for a few seconds, changed my shoes, and thought to myself, "I wonder why "T" is just standing out here?" This thought didn't get much attention because I immediately remembered that it was New Year's Eve/Day, and he could have been just coming in, as I was just coming in. A sigh of relief came over me, knowing that I didn't have to hurry. He was someone that I knew.

"T" was a young man that dated an acquaintance from high school. They shared an apartment in the adjacent building. I initiated a quick hello with a slight exchange of words in passing. While walking, I was distracted by a noise behind me near a bush that lined my stairwell, coupled with the sound of my pager going off. Having looked down at the pager to determine who it was, I found the other noise to be "T" who'd walked up behind me. Startled, I turned in his direction to let him know he'd caught me off guard. He immediately apologized and asked if he could use my phone.

After a couple of seconds of calming down, I recognized the number in my pager to be that of my sister, who I had forgotten, expected me to meet her at church that night, "T," and I proceeded up the stairs to my apartment. I unlocked the door and thought, let me make a quick call sharing my regrets. I walked in, with him still standing in the doorway, and grabbed the cordless phone from its base, on my bar.

The apartment, reasonably small, no more than 700 square feet, allowed me to make a quick dash to my bedroom door to drop the other things I was carrying down on the floor. I finished the call and remembered, by now I'm sure my cousin is worried, so let me call her to follow up, to let her know I was safe. I told her to come over the next day for dinner. After a quick recap of the events from the night, I ended the call. "T" stood still, in the cracked doorway, now slightly across the threshold. I handed "T" the phone and took a seat on the sofa cushion opposite the door where he was still standing. He'd made back-to-back calls, and as a result, I could hear a "non-working number" recording on the other end. His final attempt was the dull sound of ringing with no answer. He eventually handed me the phone back and, to my surprise, sat down beside me on the sofa.

I thought, what on earth is he sitting here for, I hadn't extended an invitation, it's 3 am. I was growing weary of fatigue. No sooner than me informing him that I was getting ready to lock up or to ask him what else he needed, "T" struck me with his fist, in my face, possibly with as much strength as he was physically able. In total shock, I immediately grabbed his hand to block the next oncoming punch and tried fending him off. I screamed and repeatedly called his name, asking him over and over what he was doing. He ignored me, delivering blow after blow, punch after to punch. It was then when I realized that I was going to have to fight back.

Confused and somewhat disoriented, I noticed that I still had the telephone in my left hand, I turned my body in and angled to turn it on, in an attempt to dial 9-1-1. In doing this, all the while, I was kicking, screaming, and fighting. Although thinly built, I was pinned down on the sofa from the weight of his frame. I had every intention of hitting every button close to 9, 1, and 1 as possible. I eventually lost control of the phone during the struggle, screaming louder and louder, continuously negotiating for my life, realizing that he was not responding to my plea, I knew then that I was in for a real fight.

As I turned to fend him off with both hands, the struggle became more intense, especially when I noticed a sharp edge coming towards my face. I quickly grabbed the dominant wrist that held the object, but not before there was a puncture to the left side of my face, temporarily blinding me with the blood that exited the wound, ultimately causing blurred vision.

At this time, I am trying to block each attempted stab. This now became his source of assault. He also tried to gain an upright position on the couch and then to the floor. Still holding his hand and trying to follow his motion or the object became next to impossible. Letting out bloodcurdling screams, regurgitating in between, now knowing that it was more than just a fit of rage and what started as a fistfight, I now had to figure out how to save my life.

I offered money, keys, cars, and anything that I thought he would have wanted to ease his desire to hurt me. He continued to wrestle with my small frame as I was able to stand, and with each attempt to run and break loose, he'd continue wounding me. This time it was repeated to my ear canal. What I thought were mere punches was later determined stab wounds.

The entire setting had become extraordinarily messy, and the screams were faint, but the will to live grew more substantial, and it was then that I started to call on the name of Jesus. I screamed over and over, "In the Name of Jesus! In the Name of Jesus!" as he continued to stab me. Amid the commotion, lamps fell off end tables, and pillows went flying.

Shivering, bloody, wounded, and in shock, I started to feel the resonation of pain turn into numbness. I instantly thought of my unanswered screams and, with little vision intact, noticed a massive pool of blood in front me resulting from episodes of regurgitating. Still, in the spirit of prayer, I felt the coach of the Holy Spirit tell me to remain calm, to slow myself down, and ultimately to use the pool of blood to pretend to be dead or at least dying so that he would leave with the belief that his mission was accomplished.

I remember telling my friends years prior if ever I were in a situation where there was blood involved, I'd pretend I was wounded and play dead.

Although this time, there was no pretending. I fell within the pool, laying prostrate on the floor, slowing my breathing down to a faint pant. Still somewhat able to see his actions from my right peripheral, I then closed my eyes. Only to notice that he'd gotten down on the floor with me. My adrenaline was that of a raging bull. I continued to pant very slowly; I was now able to see a mere shadow of him lying alongside my grotesque body. As if this experience couldn't get any worse, it did.

He then decided to disrobe me from my waist down. My heart began to race and was immediately met with the fear of sexual assault. While lying on the floor, my body was somewhat in an angle, exposing my left breast. He leaned in and kissed it, and I began to grit my teeth at the gory chill this sent down my spine.

It was then my internal cries, exited with a scream, "JESUS PLEASE HELP ME!!!" He, I'm sure amazed at the strength, took the same object he'd use to stab me and jammed me so hard in the head and said, "BITCH, Jesus can't help you, shut up and DIE!" He was immensely angered and held the object in place for seconds to make sure it did what it was supposed to do, kill me.

I took a deep gasp and for a few seconds thought, maybe this is it. I closed my eyes, and instantly the glimpse of my son's pictures on the fireplace mantle positioned behind me started to appear before me. It was as if they were placed right in front of me. I realized that seeing my son's pictures was the reassurance that I should live and not die.

When my son was born, I was 19 years old. I immediately knew that God had given me the responsibility to care for him and to see to it that he would be able to always depend on me That He would grant me the desire to see him grow up and become a prosperous adult. This became my daily prayer and, for years, continued to be, as I proudly wore the crown of a mother.

That night, I would recite that prayer and see his face over and over as I laid in a pool of blood. Within seconds, I would hear sirens, and apparently, I was the only one that would listen to them, as he was too busy prepping himself to assault me sexually.

He'd leaned back on his knees and removed his pants from his waist down and began to masturbate. The sounds of the sirens would grow louder and louder, to match the motions of his actions to prepare to penetrate me.

More noises became prevalent, such as the sound of footsteps running up the stairs. I could hear them and, most importantly, recognize that he didn't, because of his current focus. So I continued, consciously to pray within, and hope that the sounds that I was hearing were not in vain. The next noise we'd collectively hear would be the slamming of my apartment door. The Lancaster, Texas police department had received a dispatch to aide me. I later found out that the 9-1-1 called I attempted was successful, and every account of my plea for help was recorded. The commotion at the door startled the attacker. During a reasonable pursuit, the officer would have chosen not to tamper or enter the apartment, which is standard protocol. Being the only officer on the scene, I'm sure that he had some fear. After all, he was jeopardizing his safety.

This time his choice was different. He had witnessed "T" preparing himself to rape me and just couldn't allow him to follow through. He didn't know if there were other people involved, nor was he aware of the number of victims and assailants.

28

But he was able to see us on the floor and had to think quickly.

Hurriedly, "T" jumped up, began to robe himself, and pushed his body against the door, in an attempt to keep the officer from entering. Having an underlying burst of energy, I screamed at the top of my lungs. "Help me! Help me!" I cried out. As "T" ran past me into the bedroom, the officer finally entered the apartment in pursuit. He yelled, asking me where he went, and I said, "He's in the bedroom."

I was still very coherent and able to get up and run to a neighbor's apartment. I banged relentlessly on her door, screaming her name.

She and I considered each other like sisters, so there was no hesitation in opening her door. The officer ran back to my doorway and proceeded down the stairs, where he later found the backup pursuit apprehending "T" who had just jumped from the second-story window of my bedroom. He fell right into their arms as they walked up the breezeway to assist the first responding officer.

I sat outside on the cold concrete, to avoid taking my bloody mess into my neighbors' apartment. The night quickly grew long. However, all of what took fourteen minutes felt like a lifetime. She observed me in the most peculiar but calm manner. She said, "Mecka, who did this to you?" I said, "T," "T," did this, and I don't know why." In utter disbelief, my only concern was that she calls my father, my brother, and then my cousin for help. I started to shiver as I proceeded to give her their numbers. She started to dial but stopped. She ran to get some towels, and when she returned to the door, another mutual acquaintance had made her way to the door. However, she wasn't as calm. She immediately went into hysterics and mumbled obscenities and the word scissors. Because she instantly changed the tone of my emotions, feeling, and believing that I had been in a terrible fight and maybe cut a few times, but nothing this horrible, I yelled at her and asked her to please calm down. Not knowing that she'd just witnessed nothing short of the remnants of sheer horror. She covered her face that was full of tears, and I dropped my head.

By now, my dad was on the phone, and I could only say, "Daddy, please help me." My friend was now being instructed to take the phone from me by the paramedics. She continued to place the other calls that I'd asked her to. The paramedics began to prep me for my ride to the hospital. I was placed on a seated chair gurney, with a c-collar stabilizing my neck, and vividly remember looking into the sky, saying to myself, "What on earth just happened?" By now, the entire apartment complex was outside gawking, and I'm sure wondering the same thing. The gurney flattened and rolled quickly past the patrol car that "T" was sitting in.

As the ambulance proceeded to leave, I started to ask the first responders several questions. They remained soothing and calm and repeatedly said, "Miss Grate, you are going to be just fine; you're doing great!" Gauges and towels were my new wardrobe as I was disrobed adequately for the hospital, and constraints were in place to secure me for speed and a potentially bumpy ride. I remember hearing the discussion about the hospital they'd take me to. I jumped in and said, take me to the best hospital for trauma, not even having a clue the extremities of my condition.

In the small city of Lancaster, there was a local hospital that didn't have the best of ratings, and at that very moment, I was totally against them stopping there. I told them to take me to Parkland Memorial Hospital. Parkland is the County Hospital for the city of Dallas and all surrounding counties. Having noticed that I was pretty adamant, they followed my wishes.

During the route, there were three paramedics, two riding in the front of the ambulance, and one in the back. The paramedic that rode in the back with me was mesmerized and had changed a whole new shade of pigment, after assisting me and preparing me for the hospital. He was very poised, but I could tell petrified at what had just occurred. He did his best to speak to me in an uplifting tone and made every conscious effort to prepare me for the hospital. He then commenced dispatching the hospital to let them know we were on our way. After announcing his unit, he continued by saying, "We're bringing in a 24-year-old female, with multiple stab wounds, a pair of scissors protruding out of her left ear, her vitals are stable...."

The rest faded out.

I remember repeating to myself first and then to him, "Did you just say I had a pair of scissors in my ear?!" He instantly utilized his training and ability to calm and nurture. I'm sure fearing I'd freak out or raise what was still considered my average blood pressure. I'm sure he was wondering how I was still coherent and able to talk, and at this point, so did I. Despite this information, all kinds of crazy thoughts entered my mind. I was at a loss for words, but that didn't shut me up. I started to talk to him, and before you know it, I was rattling. I thought if I'd be quiet, I may not ever speak again, so I talked the entire ride.

Upon arrival at the hospital, I remember the back doors to the ambulance swinging open fast, and the next voice I heard was that of my daddy. He must have taken a plane because I was later told that he'd made it to the scene at my apartment. Yet, he was standing at the ambulance doors as soon as we arrived.

He cried out, "OH MY GOD!"

Now, this is the normal expected response for someone who is completely taken back by such a condition. But I'd never heard my daddy lose his cool. And when I heard him cry out, I thought to myself, this has got to be extremely bad.

I immediately turned into daddy's little girl and began to whimper, but for some reason, the strength that I was still able to maintain wouldn't allow me to fret. I'm still convinced it was the coaching of the Holy Spirit that allowed me to remain calm and conscious.

As I entered the jam-packed emergency room, I closed my eyes to keep from acknowledging all of the staring faces. Fifty or more doctors and nursing swarmed me. The registration department bombarded my dad with questions. They thought that I was unconscious. I then began answering my questions. The doctors couldn't believe that I was coherent enough to respond. I really didn't feel a lot of pain. My body was in total shock.

The news spread quickly, and within an hour, I was told the emergency room waiting area was full of my family and friends, unaware if they'd soon be delivering their final goodbyes. Before I had any idea how severe it was, when I initially told my friend to call my family, I had explicitly asked that they not contact my mom right away. She and my stepfather were at home, he was nursing a broken leg, and I didn't want her to worry about me. Besides, I didn't want her to have to share this with my 4-year-old son. His 5th birthday was coming the very next Saturday, and I was determined to stay on task to celebrate him.   However, by the time I'd reached the hospital, my mom was already en route. My son stayed behind with my stepfather.

With each daunting moment passing by, my symptoms became a reality, and pain starting to set in. I knew then I was in excellent care, and all my comfort and support were at my reach, allowing my faculties to all respond. I was now affixed to an examination room full of bewildered doctors rotating in and out. No one could seem to believe that I was alive or even awake for that matter. Stunned and concerned, I remember hearing the head surgeon stand at the head of the bed, sharing with my parents what the prognosis was after several hours of testing, to include MRI's and CT Scans. He stated, "We have to be very cautious, Tamecka has a pair of scissors lounged 6 inches deep in head and the same way they went in, is the same way we need to focus on taking them out."

The scissors are leaning on major veins and arteries, and one slight mishap could have paralyzed me, damage my brain, or, at worst, kill me. To mention, my eyesight was questionable, and so was the hearing of the left ear that the scissors had entered. So much to take in and digest, but my faith never wavered.

My dad, who is the epitome of unwavering faith, told the doctors, "We're going to trust that God has already started the healing, and she is on her way to recovery. You perform the surgery, and we will pray that God's hand will orchestrate it. Bring her back to us." I took a deep sigh, looked at him and then at my mom, and smiled and told them not to worry. It would be alright.

My brothers, uncles, and most of the men in my life at that time were not as tranquil. My oldest brother was beyond emotional. He cried, and he cried some more. My other two brothers were plotting to find the person who did this to me. So much so, the authorities had to soothe the scene.

By the time they were done, the alliance had formed to post "T's"" bond and assassinate him if possible. I also found out that before I'd arrived, my cousin, who was with me that night had made it to the crime scene, weapon in hand, only to locate "T" and finish him off. The entire waiting room was in an emotional upheaval.

My parents spent time consoling everyone and giving them updates. During the wait, my dad was deemed the spokesman and unmitigated counsel. He would prepare everyone for the inevitable. Each time someone would come in to visit with me, I could hear him at the door say, "Now it looks pretty bad, but with your support and her attitude, it's really not as bad as it seems, stay strong." No matter who he would give these instructions to, it never failed. The conversations would start, "Hey Mecka, how are you feeling?" I would respond, "Okay," with a half-smile, and the next thing you know, they're crying uncontrollably and out the door they went.

I understood the reactions. I didn't expect anything less. I was told that my head had swollen as big as a tire on a car. And I was starting to become unrecognizable. This went on for hours. It was when my mother re-entered the room that the weakness of my flesh began to set in. I used every muscle left working to fight back the tears. I noticed that she was at a loss of words, so I started talking to her to let her know that I was going to be okay. She then realized that she was at a point of losing it, kissed me, and left the room. I knew her heart was broken, just like mine would have been having I not be able to see my son again.

I remember shortly after that, having to agree to meet with detectives. They needed to speak with me while I was still coherent to get the most accurate account of the night's events. I talked to them in detail, sharing everything only to see how amazed they were with my memory. The strength I had was incredible.

Thirteen hours had passed, and it was time for surgery. By now, corporate prayer had been extended, and all phone calls had been made. I was wheeled down a hallway where I could see the emergency room wall lined with all my family; moms, dads, brothers, grandmas, uncles, aunts, cousins, sisters, my old high school cheerleading squad, football players, college classmates, old boyfriends, new boyfriends, if I knew them, they were there. I can remember hearing the nurse say, "We're running out of room. You've got people everywhere." From time to time, she would come into the room I'd been in and tell me how many people had arrived, and then she'd make a joke about not having enough space for patients. The love and support were immeasurable.

As I passed each face, one with a faint smile and tears, I returned the sentiment but with a thumbs up.

Recovery Equals Victory

The next day I would wake to find out that the surgery was a success.

Although acutely aware of my surroundings, I didn't know what time it was or what day it was. I just knew that I was still alive. My breathing was with the help of a machine, tubes were everywhere, with beeping sounds echoing off the walls. I began to look around, and it dawned on me the night before had happened. In and out of consciousness from anesthesia, I remember looking for my parents. I started to fret, becoming that of a little girl all over again. The nurse in the ICU noticed that I was regaining consciousness and summoned the doctors on staff. They were so excited. She began shouting with a tone as if I were deaf, "Hello Sunshine! Do you know where you are?" I responded with a slight nod. The doors of the Intensive Care Unit opened wide as my parents rushed through them. They had been looking through the double door windows the entire time, noticing the commotion with the nurses and doctors. It was then when they realized I was awake and entered the room. Their first reactions were mixtures of a sigh of relief and great big smiles. I then noticed several others standing in the doorway, waiting their turn to come in. I tried to return the laughs, but the medication and evident pain wouldn't allow for it. So, I just stared. I was attached to so much medical equipment, means of movement were impossible. The room appeared to be spinning, and all I could do was close my eyes. I immediately reopened them to make sure it wasn't a dream.

I had more company than the policy would allow for critical patients, and the frustration of not being able to talk because of the tube insertion brought about discouragement. I was compromised by medical equipment.

A group of friends was now at my beside, and I wanted to talk, so I would use my falsely manicured nails to tap on the railing for yes and no answers. Then I motioned for someone to get me a pen and paper. Not much progress came from this, but I scribbled enough for them to make out that I was okay and ready to go.

With each hour, I was met with the routine of the attending nurse, "Tamecka, hello sweetie, how are you?" I closed my eyes even tighter. I knew that it was time for my drill. Question after question, "Do you know where you are?" "Do you know how old you are?" "Do you know what day it is?" After realizing that there was no escaping them, I responded with several nods.

After napping, I woke with a spirit of determination, and I wanted to prove to myself that I could do more than just nod my head. I looked to the left of my bed and noticed the pen and paper that was given to me earlier, sitting on a table. I began to tap on the bed railing, and the nurse turns around. I pointed to the pen and paper, and she handed it to me. I looked at her to see if she was going to wait and see what I was going to do with it, and she did. I then began to write my name. At first, it was scribble. She then encouraged me to try again. I only had one hand free to write with, so she assisted by stabilizing the pad. I began to write again, and this time it was somewhat legible. She looked at the pad and said, "Very good, I understand, it's your name." This was the first time that I remembered smiling without pain. Days of intense pain and eagerness were ahead, and although I wasn't as prepared for them as I thought I would be, I was determined to see them.

As the day grew long, in and out of sleep and socializing against the better judgment of my caregivers, I felt horrible, but I knew the inner me wouldn't give up. I continued to sleep.

A few hours later, I was graced with the presence of many family and friends. As they came in by twos and sometimes fours, I would be excited to show them that I could write. I had the gestures down to the point that I knew exactly how to let them know what I wanted. I wrote like a first-grader, but I knew with time, it would get better. Everyone was excited to see the progress and effort towards my recovery. Even with this progress, came pain.

Day three mirrored day two, however, with less equipment. After my condition started to improve, the breathing machine was extubated, and I was able to talk. My throat felt horrible, and my words were faint, but the ability to verbally speak was intact, which made me very happy.

My dad and mom would come in and out of the ICU area that I was assigned, taking turns assisting with hygiene and other nurse worthy tasks. My brothers were seemingly back to their joking and teasing ways, and although I still felt like I'd been brutally jumped, I knew I was improving. My son was with my grandmother, who offered to keep him until further notice, I just didn't want him to see his mom in this condition.

The doctors had shared with everyone that what they had just experienced was nothing short of a miracle. The head surgeons' exact words were, "There's no way, I MEAN NO WAY, in a million years, you could put something this large and this sharp into someone's head and it not leave significant damage." He followed that with, "She's got to be doing something right, and someone was watching over her. It's a miracle, A MIRACLE!"

We were all just as astounded. But having been reared with our faith, we knew that there was nothing too hard for God.

After making the doctor rounds, I was improving in record time and moved to a regular hospital room the very next morning.

Chapter 2

Lights, Camera, Fate

B y now, it's day four, and all the media outlets had gotten a full account of what happened. I was in my hospital room, full of visitors, and the phone was continuously ringing.

It was my first day with only an IV for fluids, so I was able to sit up and talk. However, I didn't realize that I'd have to do the amount of talking that was in store. I remember hearing my mom say, "This is too much," and I asked her what she was talking about. She was referring to the phone traffic that the switchboard was enduring. One of the nurses and social workers had shared that the volume of calls to my room had increased tremendously. It was too much for the customer service team to handle. Calls were stemming from media outlets across the globe. Locally every news station wanted to speak with me concerning my attack. Having a room full of guests made it extremely hard, primarily since the door was revolving. I'd already spoken with the local newspaper, along with my brother and parents, so I told my mom I'd take one more call, and after that, they could redirect the traffic. The last media call was from WFAA Channel 8 news. I spoke with a journalist by the name of Gary Reaves, one of the most visible in the industry. He was very intuitive and nurturing. He asked if I was up to sharing my story, and it was then that I took a moment and a profound glimpse into why my account was deemed so remarkable.

Sure, I remember hearing that I'd had a pair of scissors in my head, but I guess it didn't register to me how miraculous it was until I witnessed the response of all who either had seen it or had heard.

Mr. Reaves asked, "Do you know that you are a "Walking Miracle"? I listened, and with hesitation shared, yes, I know God spared my life, and it was only Him who could do so. He agreed and went on to share that it was the main talk in the media. I looked at the phone and thought, well, I'm in the hospital, so I'm sure this isn't the first-time life has been saved.

Then it hit me!

The entire world, or at least those who believed, sees me as a person that would have never made it, had I not had my faith. I was reminded by the surgeons, who repeatedly said, "There's no way in a million years, this could happen again, and someone survives." Then I started to think of the fact that I had never heard a doctor who didn't take credit for saving a life, on top of sharing a stance in faith. This is a real big deal, and they aren't even ashamed to admit that God is real. So, I sat up in my bed, and I told "My Story."

As the afternoon grew longer, I'd have a wave of guests, then a wave of hospital personnel come in and out of my room.

Both to do what they came in to do, check on Tamecka. Then I noticed a lady who I hadn't seen before. She introduced herself as a social worker, with her arm loaded with pamphlets and information for a mental evaluation. I thought to myself, "I don't need that, GOD saved me!" I wasn't rude to her, but I quickly shared that I was fine, taking her information and card and sending her on her way. My mom looked at me and said, "It's okay if you talk to someone in this field to help," and I told her, "I'm good."

My primary focus was to get better and get home to my son. Looking back in hindsight, I should have taken every opportunity to seek counsel to better prepare me for "Life After."

My stay so far had been full of moments of awe. My hearing test had remarkable and better results than expected with no issues. My eye was fully intact, with just a slight impairment called strabismus, (crossed-eyed horizontally vs. vertically). However, with a slight twist to my neck, my vision instantly became aligned, I'd later have this corrected.

There was one setback that caused me to wonder if I'd be able to function physically at 100%. The stabbing in my neck area had damaged the pilot between my nose and throat, making it extremely hard to guide and swallow without choking or suffocation while drinking or eating. I grew tired of trying to figure it out, so I opted not to eat or drink. This experience was terrifying, and for the first time, I started to feel defeated. The nurses would explain that the area in which I suffered the damage was shared and, with time, would repair itself. But I loved to eat, and I had already lost weight from the stay in ICU, so I started to worry.

I then was introduced to a nutritionist who shared several thickening supplements that were used to exercise the muscle but taste horrible. This was the first time I started to cry. My mom and brother just happened to be visiting during this time and was just as frustrated for me. They asked if there were any dietary restrictions and the nutritionist stated no, they just wanted me to be able to swallow without it coming back through my nose. I made a joke and said, "If it were a root beer float, I'd be able to get it down because it tastes good." My brother retorted, "I'll go get you a float, let's try and see."

Astoundingly, root beer float became the diet and choice, and in no time, my pilot regained its strength. I was slowly eating soft to solid foods and drinking drinks with consistency were doable. Over time my diet returned to normal, miracle after miracle.

My article with the local newspaper was set to print for reading the next day, and I was anxious to see how the story would be portrayed. My mom had shared with them a recent picture of me. Ironically, about a month before the attack, my son and I had taken family portraits. My brother gave his version of what to expect, based upon his interview, and so did my parents. We all were wondering, just what would the world have to say. Saturday morning arrived, and the paper hits the shelves. "Woman survives brutal stabbing attack" on the first page of the Metropolitan section of the paper, to be continued onto another page for more details. The article gave a full account of the story from my view and the view of my family.

Before the release, the phone traffic had died down, and I was able to retake calls in my room. However, this day started a new era. The article pushed the trend of curiosity all over again, and the phone began to ring nonstop. Calls stemmed from as far as other countries, with translators. The worldwide news entities, such as CNN, had gotten wind and was able to share their version of the story of a 24-year-old female who survived a pair of scissors being stabbed 6 inches deep, from one side of her head to the other. She's a Miracle. The other local news stations started soliciting phone interviews, but I refused, so they journaled their versions, by way of different markets. I was taken back by the attention and decided that it was too much for me to handle, especially while trying to recover.

The doctors and nurses, some not assigned to me, even came in and started to tell me I was a "celebrity." I was very humbled by the support, but far from flattered by the attention. All I wanted to do was go home to my son and cook that long-awaited meal I initially intended the night before it happened. Plus, it was his 5th birthday, and I couldn't imagine being away from him to help him celebrate. And although my grandmother and the rest of my family would give him a party that day, I was left with no choice. Very saddened, I closed my eyes and tried to sleep. To say that I was overwhelmed was an understatement.

Sunday morning arrived, and my parents were at my bedside. Guests were still fluid, calls continued, and my desire to go home grew more and more. After numerous X-rays and MRI's, it was determined that I'd been healed in record timing and was only there for final assessment and observation before I would be discharged. The Head surgeon and attending doctors were very impressed, and the social workers and other administration were left speechless. I was due to be released in a couple of days. I received flowers, cards, candies, and stuffed animals from all over the world. The nurse had them tucked away for me because the room was just too crowded. Each time I received a token, she'd show me and then take it to its new home until I would be able to leave.

One week later, the hospital began starting the process to release me to go home. The thought of going home brought on excitement like never before. However, it wasn't to my apartment. I was now moving back with my parents. My family moved my belongings from the former residence, now deemed a crime scene. Having been on my own for a couple of years at that point, it was bittersweet but consoling to know that I'd be in the company of loved ones. I knew it would help me fully process the last week and prepare for the future.

I'd spend the day practicing how I would approach my five-year-old son. How do you explain being away for eight days and no sign of mommy, besides missing his birthday party? And although I made it my business to talk to him every day, I knew there would be a lot of questions, and I couldn't tell him there was an unfortunate accident. I was extremely petrified about how to share with him his new mommy.

Besides, my appearance had changed, and I didn't know how he'd take it. I still looked a little like a horror film rejects, and I honestly didn't want to scare him. Even being that small, he trusted me, and I had to make good with him.

The following Tuesday morning, I was discharged from the hospital, in tow with boxes and boxes of goodies. Who would have thought that their entire life would change so drastically yet, miraculously? Beyond thankful at another chance at life, I knew it would be different. I didn't realize how much so. Dressed to impress in a pair of hospital scrubs, that I kept as memorabilia, I looked back at the automatic doors, holding a vase, while smelling the roses.

Both Sides Of Accountability

In the days and months ahead, I'd find myself continuously talking with detectives and judicial personnel to give an account of what happened the early morning of New Year's Day, to determine the fate of the man who was responsible for trying to take my life. I knew he was still incarcerated and being held at the Dallas County Jail, and the time would soon come to meet with him face to face. Interview after interview, with authorities, prosecutors, and the district attorney, would enlighten me more than I'd ever care to be involved, and a trip to the forensic sciences building for DNA testing didn't excite me either. Nevertheless, I knew I had to do what was expected of me to see to it that justice would prevail. It was my duty to society and myself to prevent this from happening to anyone else. May 1996, the trial would begin. News stations all over the country would capture and share the daily updates of the woman now deemed "Miracle." After four days of intense and emotional testimony, from myself and other witnesses, "T" was charged with attempted capital murder and sentenced, on May ninth, my twenty-fifth birthday, to Life in Prison. Moving past this day and looking into the days ahead afforded me the chance to focus on rebuilding my life, but first, I had to learn to accept it, and with this came the determination to face Life After.

Chapter 3

Doses of Grace and Mercy

After being discharged from the hospital, days of wound healing of the body, mind, and spirit would take on a new approach. If fear had to set in, this would have been the time. I can remember leaving the hospital with so many questions. Questions that would stem from taking care of my wounds to physical setbacks and the discomforts that came with it. I'd also be reminded with a daily glimpse in the mirror that my appearance had changed. And with this would come questions from others. It was a lot to digest. Aside from the physical adjustments, my ability to think all of this through, became a chore, moments of replaying the scenes of the attack in my head would pull away more mental time than I would have wanted to give in to. With each step, I'd lean on my spirit man, who I'd questioned more than a few times.

Pondering often in sheer disbelief.

Asking myself the question over and over, "Did this really happen to me?", with the answer "yes" returning each time. As with anything, time became my natural healing source. Being receptive to the attention brought on by the attack was also a way to get through those moments. I could have quickly shut the entire world out with hopes my life would go on. But I ultimately knew that I'd continue to relive it if I hadn't faced it. Being open and transparent to this new normal, were the keys to conquering the overall fear in my mind and the shame that accompanied my unique appearance.

With each moment, I would revisit the different parts of the ordeal to try to make sense of it. I'd replay in my head over and over, what is it that I could have done differently to avoid the attack. Did I have any warning signs? Every day there was more and more that entered my mind. Yet, I didn't want to consume myself thinking about it, so I would make it my business to bring on as much as regular activity as possible.

School was getting ready to start for my son, who was headed back to kindergarten, after being on winter break, and that gave me a reason to stand up in my mommy shoes and do what I needed to do to prepare him and not think about it as much. As expected, he'd spend a great deal of time asking me about my injuries, especially my eye. I'd given him a very brief summary of what took place, leaving out as many gruesome details as possible. He began to take pride in his mommy, having won this fight of his imagination. I agreed with him, and he'd smile with honor, just happy to have his mommy back.

Ultimately, my concern was getting back to as normal as possible. Normal to me meant being a mom without constraints, I'd pride myself in my ability to do so and to think that a tragic ordeal could change this scared me more. Being incapable of caring for myself, along with not being able to care for my son, was petrifying, and I was determined not to allow fear to author my days. For a while, I'd look at my injured eye and then my other eye and make a comparison. I couldn't believe that my face had changed, along with my vision. Exercising my eyes, expression after expression wouldn't help, and I'd soon find myself oppressed at the idea of this being a permanent look for me. But the spirit of thankfulness always seemed to creep up on me just as I would try to feel sorry for myself. I was blessed that my eye was still intact, and I was still able to see clearly. Although it required a slight bend in my neck to keep my vision straight, I was confident in knowing this wouldn't prevent me from taking care of my son and me or the ability to appreciate the "Beauty of my Scar."

Don't Be Afraid to Revisit That Day

The calls and visits were still pretty prevalent, leaving little time to dissect my thoughts. And although I was afraid of the space any idle time could afford, I welcomed the moments of solace that were extended over time. I was taken back by each gesture, one, and the same.

But these moments didn't stop at calls or visits. I'd received so much mail from the hospital. Each day I would take the time to read through message after message. I'd come across the sweetest token of love from an elderly lady who sent a beautiful card with a note and a five-dollar bill. At the end of her note, she told me to buy myself plenty of snacks while I healed.

And all I could think was, this had to be the sweetest gesture for her even to consider sending money to a stranger, money of great value, thus the term "plenty." I knew she was elderly because she shared in her note, that in the 80 years she's lived, she'd never been so thankful for God sparing someone else's life.

Moments like this kept me motivated.

So much so the incentive and will to live would overpower the nervousness that would present itself in the alone time.

I'd allowed WFAA an exclusive interview to follow up on the telephone call during my stay in the hospital. This in-person interview was scheduled that following week, just two weeks after I was home.

The day arrived, and it started with a little bit of anxiety. Undeniably, I should have been focused on preparing to tell my story in front of the cameras, but that's not what made me edgy. I'd scheduled my hair appointment to prepare for my first in-person interview later to be shared on television with the world watching. However, I was more nervous about my hairstyle than I was the cameras! Those who know me know that my hair is my unspoken statement of fashion. My sister was my stylist during this era, and she'd make sure she captured the achievable look every time. But because of the surgery and to avoid my wounded ear from getting infected, it would be weeks before I was able to have my hair thoroughly shampooed and styled.

She'd spend a great deal of time nurturing me beforehand and took pride in knowing that I trusted her to make me happy in an area that so many others wouldn't care. Nevertheless, I wasn't sure if my hair is styled was the right focus. Maybe it was the hope that it would take the attention of my new look, the limped eye.

I wanted it all to be just right, and eventually, it was.

Journalist Gary Reaves had been in touch with my family and me since the day we spoke in the hospital and was just as eager to hear my story as I was to share it. Young and novice, I had no idea what to expect. I asked a friend to give me a ride to my dad's house, where the interview would take place. That was the first time that I was in the company of just a friend, no family, no phones.

He took on the job with pride.

While riding, I recited the story to him over and over so that he could encourage me along the way. That ride was just as unnerving as the first ride in the ambulance. To think, I was getting ready to share with the entire Metroplex what happened to me on that day. We would arrive at my dad's home, nestled in a rural setting, only to pull up to a couple of media trucks and unfamiliar cars. I saluted my friend with a hug of gratitude and went in to share "My story."

Don't Be Muzzled

After the interview had taken place, it would be scheduled to air almost a month later. And even with this window of time, there would be no break in telling "My story." The first newspaper article was still circulating, and I'd been contacted by so many others to give interviews. I spoke to interviewers and networks as far away as Istanbul, Turkey. Invitations to speak at philanthropic organizations of crime victims, domestic violence entities, churches, and other charitable affiliates, became my new regular. I'd gone back to work only to be asked to do a follow-up interview with the local paper, The Dallas Morning News, and I did. This article was titled "Woman's recovery amazes all." This article shared the miraculous recovery of my attack and further details about what I expected to do with life post this experience. I found that the more I discussed it, the more therapeutic it was.

I'd meet new people just about anywhere, every day, and this only further encouraged my extroverted ways. Even after the attack, I'd never meet a stranger. By the time I'd gone back to work, I'd regained my sense of independence, allowing me to transport myself to doctor appointments and other scheduled events. With each visit, I find myself sharing "My Story." Most of the time, it would be because someone would ask me about my scar.

Other times I'd feel God lead me to share with someone who may not have been having the best day. However, it always made me feel better when I did. Especially when I saw the response of how thankful the receiving ears would be to know that God could do such a Miraculous thing. He left me here to talk about it, and I did every chance I got.

All Health Matters – Mental and Physical

Suppressing trauma is as detrimental as its actual event.

Without the release, you tend to hoard the mental space necessary for healing—the space required to function in a healthy cognitive manner. The more you hold it in, the more it's prone to represent itself in different forms. These forms foster depression, anxiety, fear, and a host of unhealthy attributes that, over time, would ultimately contribute to the demise of the initial experience. During the earlier days post the trauma, I spend a great deal of time discussing the traumatic details. So much so, that I started to sound like a broken record. Yet, this would soon allow me to see that my story was somewhat similar, in stance, not in nature, to the accounts of so many others. At this point, sharing became therapeutic.

It posed as a filter that would strain the unwanted emotions. Not only did I find a sense of relief when I shared my story, but each opportunity also allowed me to be open to hearing someone else's account, and before long, the positive energy would mesh and whether with an audience or two strangers, you'd walk away knowing that you were better after doing so.

Chapter 4

Embrace Support With Open Arms

Although moving around became seamless, I soon find out that it would be more to this than just an invitation and an appearance.

I'd find myself needing a constant reminder that moving forward would take more action on my part. I'd have to reinvent my wheel of significance. Having gotten accustomed to the attention my experience created, somewhat push the other areas of my life into a corner of neglect. Once I realized this, I started to incorporate my old routine with my new routine, and from this came consistency. I had to remember that "me" before trauma still existed.

I was blessed to have the presence of my immediate family, along with my church family and very close friends. God knew, without them, I would have been completely lost.

You see, my dad, who is the pastor of the church I attended, born with a heart of compassion, made it his business to nurture me beyond the darkest moments. He would later share that as he was hosting the night watch service on the night of my attack, traditionally known as a service to be held on New Year's Eve at most churches for a fresh start of the new year, the task of praying beyond his normal realm would take over at that very time. He continuously prayed and prayed, stating he knew it was something that God was doing at that very moment, and he couldn't stop praying. And I know, he and the church's obedience, played a role in my survival. Just as I was calling on the "Name of Jesus," they were praying for a miracle.

My mom, being one of the most organized people I know, was a nurse without the uniform because it was embedded in her heart. She worked with my obligatory financial entities to make sure I wasn't left with the damage of thousands of dollars in medical bills. She was introduced to several resources for crime victims, and I was able to move forward without any financial burdens from my attack. Her ability to take care of my finances and any other business and personal aspects of my life was beyond thoughtful.

My brothers turned bodyguards, never left my side. They would soon begin to taunt and tease me as usual, but now with a heightened tone of protection.

My son was always my driving force, so innocent and transparent, began to love on me even harder, he'd somehow figured out that his mom had been in some danger and he wasn't going to let that happen again.

My maternal grandmother, the cast-iron fist of the family, made sure we knew how to love one another and stay involved with one another. She poured this into our family daily. She set the tone for my firmness to bounce back by making sure she never let me see her sweat. Even after I was attacked, she said with tears in her eyes, how she wished I had a weapon to take him out, but she's glad my fist, in her mind, did the job. That was the only thing she said, and I knew all of that meant I love you, and I'm glad you're still with me.

We didn't have to worry about in-home daycare because she was it and protective of us. So, there was nothing for me, my siblings, and my cousins, also raised as sisters and brothers, to spend countless days with each other. We knew we could count on one another no matter what. Every aspect of family, Uncles, and Aunts alike, was in full-blown support of making sure my life would be as ordinary as can be.

Although my list of friends would grow overnight, the core group remain intact and made sure I knew I was loved.

The embrace from my family and friends was and still is beyond supportive. My circle is vast in-crowd, but intimate in nature had always been within arm's reach. Support came seamlessly, and there was never a doubt in my mind that I would have to ever worry about this.

Seek and Ye Shall Find

I attended church regularly and even more immediately after my attack. I knew that my spiritual family was forever praying and that the one area of my life that I needed to stay on course would be with my relationship with God. I wavered in and out from time to time dealing with moments of distress and "Life," but I always remembered my basic training. The same basic training that allowed me to call on God when I knew my parents couldn't hear me that night. I've always held myself to a standard of trusting my spirit, man. However, when the ways of the world sneak up behind me, I know that I've got a shield and armor within reach.

I'm so blessed to know that I don't have it all figured out. Life is sure to present prelude after prelude of ordeals to conquer, especially after trauma. And in times of uncertainties, this is the one mindset that fully allows me to depend on God solely. My connection to him is my life's support, relationships that involve worship, prayer, fasting, and repentance.

- Worship starts at the opening of my eyes. I spend this time praising and thanking him for ALL things.
- Prayer is a daily regimen and happens in thought and spontaneity
- Fasting is necessary for staying on course when I feel my world misaligning. I implement fasting
- Repentance is my daily duty, not to be taken for granted extended by grace and mercy

There's a great deal of comfort that accompanies life challenges when I implement these steps. As they further solidify my relationship with God and reassure me when doubt starts to set in.

Professional support is available in many capacities, whether it be in an organized group or setting designed just for those who are still trying to process any chain of events. Most of the time, you find someone else's story to hug your own laterally.

Being a part of this type of support setting affords the ability to feel a part and not isolated.

Everyone has gone through something. It's always been my heart's content to be as available to all as I would want them to be for me. And although I hadn't taken on the counseling environment, I knew it was an option and exceptionally vitally important to the success of survival.

At the time of my ordeal, counseling was the first resource extended to me after surgery, and my condition became stable. I can remember the Social worker coming to my room with an arm full of pamphlets and me instantly thanking her while at the same time turning it down.

My initial response was since I was deemed "A Miracle," why would I need that. As if it would go against God's will. As I look back, I now like to think of it as "Novice and Stubborn." It's no secret that during this era, the mere introduction of counseling meant the inability to function on your own. Society had decided for me that I was beyond the need, and unfortunately, I agreed.

This may have been one of the costliest mistakes I could have ever made post-trauma. Thinking back on some of the choices I made during "Life After" has led to what I know could have been avoided had I just sought professional help. This help would have an aide in making sound judgment calls and detouring from unwarranted decision making, had I not tried to fill voids with unrealistic expectations.

You'll find those details in another book (lol sigh).

Having researched how good counseling is, and how necessary it is to live in clarity gives me comfort in sharing with everyone that will listen, how vitally important it is to seek it.

With this, I'm so blessed to know that God sustained me, having declined this resource, which I am now confident He equipped so many with its purpose.

Grieve Out Not In

Grieving comes with many masks. Nevertheless, it would be inhumane to say that I never felt any grief post my attack. When I was met with it, I went back to the stages of processing it. I made it my business to better familiarize myself with what I'd experienced. Brushing it under the rug or holding it in was never an option. I took the time to talk to me about it, coming to terms that the picture was much bigger than me. Having survived, I knew that it wasn't just a fight I'd conquered, it was a purpose I'd gained. Once I realize that the flesh, which is the primary source of control for grief, doesn't rule my day-to-day, I then opened the kit for survival. The mere ability to grieve OUT not IN is a true anecdote to surviving.

Ultimately during the grief stages post-trauma, you'll find that it is designed to change the way you view yourself, others, and the world around you. Although it is a big part of the process, it is also intricate in freeing you from the captivating thoughts that push the negative side of that plan. As written and often told, there are five stages of grief: Denial, Anger, Bargaining, Depression, and Acceptance.

Remembering your core values will help you navigate through these stages. Core values that stem from when you were little until the day of detriment and the days afterward.

The easiest of the five stages that I feel I was able to conquer is that of Anger. I never gave space to anger because I never took the trauma personally.

However, very tragic, and unnerving, to say the least, from the inception of the attack and the final sound of the gavel that concluded the attempted capital murder trial sentencing, I stood firm on the fact that death wasn't meant for me. His attempt failed and being granted a second chance at life was so much more rewarding. So, there was no need to harbor anger.

The most difficult of the five stages was that of Acceptance. Acceptance to me meant that I was fully prepared for the life presented to me after trauma, and that couldn't be any further from the truth. Especially in my novice interpretation, so instead of accepting it, I spent a great deal of time trying to avoid it. The caveat to this was how God miraculously chose to spare me, leaving me with nothing but a scar as representation of His grace and an assurance that I was left here for a reason.

I didn't have a cape to wear or a button push to avoid any of the stages, as I'm confident that I visited them all, but I did have confirmation from God that none of them would stop me from sharing my story, and the more I shared, the more the stages of grief would diminish.

Chapter 5

Accepting Life Over Death

C rime victim was a term I'd hear quite regularly. However, I never referred to myself as one.

I'd heard it on the news, I heard it with the detectives, I heard it with the judicial system, but I never allowed it to be part of my title. To be a victim or be victimized would mean I'd lose a sense of myself and purpose. Did I expect to or ask to become part of the population? No. Therefore, I never thought of myself in that manner. The more I gave myself credit for living, the more I knew that is was just that easy to do. I was recently asked during the night of my attacked did I ever think I'd die, I immediately responded, "I was too busy thinking about living." I truly believe if it were my time, then I would have expired then.

When we go through life's changes, whether traumatic or not, the critical word to reflect on is through. You come out on the other side, knowing it wasn't meant for you to stay in that condition. When you stay in a situation, then you die a slow death. When you've been giving another chance at life, then you stand a chance at living a longer life, not in time but fruitfulness.

Seek Positivity Avoid Negativity

Although I know "My Story" will never mirror that of another, I find it my pleasure in being around positive settings, not just birthdays, baby showers, weddings, or such - environments that share other life experiences. These types of parameters are the ones that foster collaboration, support, celebrating, and philanthropy. They're designed to bring out the actual narrative of a person, removing the doubt and potential vibes of temporary or negativity. It's also essential for me not to store these efforts within so that when it's time to extend myself, I can do so naturally.

I'm a firm believer that when it's not done genuinely, it forms a cloud that can go from white to black quickly. Distinguishing authenticity and faux. Not faux as in false but as in strain. The type of anxiety accompanies you when you don't feel like sharing.

Negativity is easy to entertain rather than it is to keep up with. That's why it is vitally important to start your day with positivity. The way you start your day is huge in determining the vibes that will set the tone for you and those around you. And even though you can't control how others may start their day, you can decide whether or not it meets your standard of acceptance or avoidance.

I usually start my day with my favorites, soft music, fresh air and coffee, an inspirational text, extra rest, a hug, or whatever my desire is for the day. When presented with something negative, I gladly return my time or thoughts to the start of my day, which helps me keep my focus. Remaining positive is usually more taxing and involves a little extra effort. Ways that I remain positive are by reflecting on who or what may be enduring much worse than me and counting my situation all joy. Having set expectations of myself to aspire and lift my own head up, always leads me to extend inspiration to others which is easy math for sustaining positivity.

Positivity is contagious.

Remember, your story will continue to be told. It needs to be done with as much of an encouraging brand as it can be delivered.

Give Yourself Credit

Giving yourself credit when your happiness supersedes your sadness is so essential to healing, especially after trauma. All too often, you find situations where the focus is put more on the bad days versus the good ones.

To give yourself credit means to look in the mirror and own your new truth. To liberate yourself to the point of finding the good in whatever may be attempting to redirect your thoughts.

Each time that I share my story, I find a moment to cherish how pleasing it was for me to give an account to survive, knowing that it could potentially help someone else. This type of creditworthiness is rewarding. It comes with a sense of accomplishment, leaving no room for negative dwellings.

Here are a few ways that you can give yourself credit:

- Push replay on your good days to overshadow the bad ones
- Know that your survival is an achievement and a reward
- Being "chosen" by God comes with exceptional "rating."

- Don't compare your score to anyone else, and uniqueness comes with a high credit rating

I know my survival was nothing short of a miracle, which is even more reason to believe that I was chosen to walk in a boldness that shows I have great "acclaim" with God. Not to be used in vain or in the sense of entitlement. But to be shared with others so that they too will know that their credit is just as good.

Chapter 6

Life Happens

U nderstanding that the world is emotionally flat, along with learning not to isolate yourself, are the two components that will help you see that no one is exempt from life's circumstances. The playing field is leveled daily, and no one will ever know when or if the time to endure will present itself.

When you take inventory of your life without a measuring stick, you learn that no feat is too hard for God. When you are met with curveballs, you exercise the moments of despair as quickly as possible so that you don't find yourself traveling to, "Oh me, Oh my," land. Sure, no one expects to deal with or go through some things, especially that as horrific as my story.

But when I learned that life really happens, I made a clear assessment that not only was I not exempt, the amount of strength I am expected to gain from it, positioned me for whatever may come next.

Of course, I would love to see the rainbows glow, and the flowers dance frequently. However, when the storms come, I know the rainbows and buds will form shortly after as a reassurance of lessons that were meant to learn as with another opportunity to move forward. It won't always be that easy. But, as long as easy is an option, it's worth getting to.

When life happens, try these methods to help you through the process:

Focus solely on your purpose, remember the object is equivalent to privilege

Push beyond your expectations by adding an addendum to your goals

Redirect the energy around you by sharing space in a different environment around new people and new things

Reset, Reset and Reset by remembering your why and how you were chosen to make an impact

You Are Not Alone

As astounding as many survival stories may be, you can rest assure you are not alone. Quite honestly, the survival ribbon spool has just about run out of pretty colors.

Everyone has survived something.

Whether it be a brush with death or heartbreak, there is a population. Recognizing this can either make you feel like you're a part of something sorrowful or a movement. I want to choose the latter. A movement gives you vitality, and with that, you inherit longevity.

I've been part of and witnessed many forums of survival. Although alarming, it's not surprising. The world we live in is often plagued with news that either share the demise or survival of something or someone. The population of both is probably pretty close in number. However, when the opportunity to survive has been given, you learn to take that as what we usually call a second chance. With this second chance, you make it, and you move into the dimension that promotes philanthropy.

Survival drives philanthropic efforts. Most of all, if not all, organizations, non-profits, and alike entities are rooted in that of survival.

These efforts, in turn, light the candle for continuous collaborations of those who have similar experiences. It's part of the wheel. When you realize that they're so many who have experienced life-changing events that mirror or are as astounding as your own, you learn to embrace the ideas of what was meant to be. Instead of falling victim to, "Oh my, why me?"

Why not you? Having been born with the spirit of survival and blessed with another chance is, even more, the reason why.

Don't Create a Hopeless Platform

All too often, we find ourselves pondering the "once was" through new lenses. We are determined to hold on to the life we had before our ordeal and deemed it was much more straightforward. The need to adjust becomes taxing, and all we want is to go back to a time when our new routine didn't exist. Let me be honest in saying that this has happened to me and quite often, might I add.

There are days when I want my scar to disappear, but then I'm reminded of how distinctive this scar is and its endearment.

It epitomizes daily doses of grace and mercy. With every right and even wrong, I'm constantly reminded that hopelessness is not an option, and I'm purposely here to share my story, along with just how glorious and awesome God is to have chosen me to do so.

The platform is usually accompanied by a pretense of what the world looks like without problems. It's created to make you believe that if you must deal with the issues of life, you will eventually fall victim to hopelessness.

There are many ways to avoid this. Changing the weaknesses of your mindset is one. Having been afforded a supernatural strength during the ordeal is even more reason to know that hopelessness holds no ground. Learn to take time and dissect the real reason for your survival. If losing hope was in order, then you would not have survived. Believing that you were chosen is also a way to change the stigma of hopelessness, the word says: This race is not given to the swift nor the strong but he who endures until the end (Ecclesiastes 9:11). This means you are not allowed to give up, and hope should be your source for spiritual energy. Remember it's okay to visit the gray areas of life, don't stay there.

Pull Up Your Bootstraps

Each day is a different day, and we should treat it as such. Will each day be a great day? No. However, whether it includes having to revisit the storms of life, you still must find a way to keep going. I've learned with each awakening moment that each day is a privilege. Privileges are granted, and when you know this, you tend to acknowledge it as such. Having said this, whenever you feel like your day is not worthy of your purpose, take time to pull up your bootstraps and revisit the mirror of expectation. Expectations that were embedded in you before you were even a thought. You will then realize that a new day is just another opportunity to fulfill your destiny.

The privilege of being granted another day to make good on your purpose is all the incentive you need to get up and make it happen. I'm not saying it will be easy, but I am saying it will be worth it.

Chapter 7

Trauma Does Not Define You

T he year I was attacked brought about several segments of fifteen minutes of fame. Having been featured several times on the news and other media outlets as the "Miracle Girl," "The Scissor Lady," "The Woman of extreme Faith," and many other titles, opened a whirlwind of soliciting like never before.

After the news outlets unveiled my story, phone calls from all over the world were happening. Producers from radio to television, charities, and local entities, reached out for interviews and the new normal became more abnormal than ever.

Having accepted several invitations to share my experience, brought about an entirely new revelation. I'd ask myself daily, "Am I equipped for this, or at least mature enough to handle what this world was expecting."

The invitations afforded me to travel and exposure across the country; I'd appear on some of the most name brand segments, capturing audiences across the globe. I have to admit; this didn't always set the tone for comfort. I was a 24-year-old working mom who wanted to do just that and only that. However, this was not the case and wouldn't be because of "Life After."

Sharing my story became pretty redundant, and because of my "new look", it was almost always the start of a conversation. Adapting to this was fine, but my life started to feel scripted. I never wanted my attack or the remnants thereof to define me. And although each time I would share, I'd feel a sense of therapy; I still did not want to welcome it as a daily platform.

There were times I'd share what happened, as if I were reciting it, all to get to the end, just to hear a person say, "I would never have known this if you would not have shared."

With each moment, I'd make sure that I'd let any audience know, whether it be one person or two hundred, that although I had experienced the unimaginable, I still found solace in living a fruitful yet trauma-free life. And with this, I'd soon allow others a chance to get to know me for myself, as opposed to introducing my story so that they can feel as if what happened was second nature. I can't say that there were never any moments of despair; there absolutely were. But the more I pressed towards what I knew worked for me and not the commercialism it afforded, the more transparent my life became. To prove this, I went back to work six weeks after my attack. However, this, too, became newsworthy.

Finding My Way Back

The first thing that comes to mind when you experience anything extraordinary, especially that which changes your typical day to day life, is how to get back on track. You immediately try to find a way to make it happen. The idea would be to wake up with the same routine as of the day before, but then that would be too easy. Keep in mind extraordinary can encompass many hats. The hat of excitement, uncertainty, newness, unfamiliarity, of fear, and so on. No matter the hat, there's still life after, and how you wear the hat on any given day will determine how you adjust or cope.

Since that life-altering night, so many things have happened, but that would have always been the case. With time comes change, right? Well, when that change is coupled with an extraordinary event, one that could have ended your life, you find that enjoying and/or adjusting to it takes much effort. Often returning to that day in time, remembering things as they were only if the bounce back were that easy.

After my attack, everything became a challenge, physically, emotionally, and spiritually. There were "why me" days, that were chased by "why not me" days.

With each giving moment, I had to find a level of strength that would aide in how I would move forward.

Support from others was my primary source of strength. My parents were very intricate in this. Overall, being a mother is what drove me to push that extra effort, along with the consistencies necessary to gain ground in every area of my life. I remember so vividly days after my attack, my son Jacori would be turning five. Bandaged and still hospitalized, I was determined to make sure his previously planned party would go without a hitch.

Reality hit hard when I realized that I wouldn't be in attendance for it. As the days approached, I spent time on the telephone organizing and dictating how I wanted it to be, and this was so that he wouldn't miss me being there. To protect him from the unknown, I never allowed him to see me in the hospital. However, me not being there for him, was a different feat. This became the first account of many that would change my life forever.

As the year progressed, I would find myself being consumed with the new challenges of doctor visits, physical impairments, mothering, shared living space, making a living. And the biggest challenge of it all, being a survivor of attempted capital murder, known to many as the miracle girl. Even with this, I knew there was still "Life After."

A few people in my life during this time stood with me and kept me within sanity's reach. One in mainly, who was a great friend at the time, became my right hand and constant armor-bearer. During and after my hospital stay, there wasn't a day that went by that he didn't call or come to see me to make sure I wasn't in need. He didn't know it at the time, but his presence afforded me the comfort of knowing that I was cared for in such a way that if my life had to change. He was willing to see his change along with it.

Our time together increased, and the fondness was inevitable. I remember sharing with him over that first year that everything was going so fast and that I didn't understand how to cope with it, but as much as I didn't want to accept my new normal, he was there to show me it was going to be okay.

What started as a giddy friendship in no time, we turned into an interest of love. He then became my daily sounding board, and with this came a stable relationship. The following year we'd marry and welcome our son, and twenty-five months later we welcomed our daughter, life was finally getting back to normal. Although we experienced the downfalls and issues of any relationship, no problem ever seemed as big as the one that presented itself on the first day of the prior year. This union was built on endurance, and we welcomed it and called it our glue.

Normalcy started to present itself, and with each day, came adjustments. The strength that I would gain from this was unfathomable. Yet, knowing that I had an entire world in awe of my survival, I'd find myself spending more time letting others know it was, by no means, by any chance, that I would take credit for what I know only God could do.

Remembering Your Goals

As a mother, now wife, life started to chime in. I'd changed careers, with three small, actively involved children; my self-employed husband was very intricate in their daily tasks. This allowed me to focus on the goals that I'd set years before my attack. One main goal going forward was to give so much of myself that no one would ever feel the need to treat me any differently post my ordeal. But also recognizing the enormous amount of strength I'd gained just getting "life after" what I considered under control.

As I matured, sharing my story became more viable, and when I think about it, this is when I realized its sole purpose was to share with others what life could look like after such a horrific ordeal.

This was it!

To share my authentic self, without displaying the mental bumps and bruises that generally post-trauma, no mask just authenticity. Being myself gave me the will and strength to share. There are so many others who have experienced life-changing situations and have never understood or embraced the ability just to be themselves.

After being exposed to a world that was eager to applaud my survival, I initially was challenged with the emotions that came with keeping up with the expectations of others. When all along, all I desired to be was me.

As the years progressed, I didn't feel a need to share my story at the point of entry. I continued to allow people to get to know the "Tamecka" that so many others already knew. The strategy here was to be so purposeful in my ability to move on, that even with my scar, the miracle would still hold its power.

As for my prior goals, the company I worked for offered college tuition aide, allowing me to go back to school, without the financial strain, to earn my degree even as a full-time employee. This was one of the most rewarding achievements that I could have ever received.

Especially at the witness of my children who saw firsthand how to persevere and meet essential goals, post-traumatic experience.

Re-Introducing Yourself to You

After making a pat to myself to complete my desired goals, I also took the time to reintroduce myself to me. With this introduction came lots of personal time. I traveled, shopped, cooked, and joined many organizations. Although simple to most, this was the incentive that allowed me to reinvent my wheel to move forward. I met new people and reacquainted with old friends. It was doing this era in my life that I realized I was blessed with a spirit of discernment of trust. No matter who I met or where we were, I'd find myself engulfed in the likenesses of life. That transparency immediately fostered a stable relationship, and the ability to soothe and extend compassion where the need is was seamless.

Another purposeful, Ah-ha moment.

To think, God left me here for His people.

To share his goodness and to be so transparent in doing so, that whoever's path I'd cross, they'd see the HIM in me and gain some sense of hope.

Resonating with this comfort would then allow those who trusted me to revisit their circumstance, with a birds-eye view. You see, even with all that I'd previously experienced, many of life's curveballs still managed to make it my way, and I then realized it was solely for times such as these. There's a sense of passion that comes with being able to relate to others. "Me too" is a movement beyond all things, and it feels good when you can assure someone else that they are not alone. Kindred closes the gaps in testimonies, and for this reason, I know that there's life that happens, and there's "Life After."

Here are a few ways that you can re-introduce yourself to you:

- Take personal time out for yourself, away from others
- Try something that you've never tried before
- Set and complete a long-awaited goal
- Journal and date your thoughts and revisit for growth at a later date

Chapter 8

You Were Chosen

❦

" "**F**or if you remain silent at this time, relief and deliverance will arise for the Jews from another place, and you and your father's house will perish. And who knows whether you have not attained royalty for such a time as this." When I first heard this scripture, I thought it was all about being the incentive that came along with being blessed during a particular time in life. However, after witnessing the bumps and bruises that accompanied spiritual growth, I was allowed to digest the full context, then realizing it was a reprimand to Esther. It went along with self-preservation and self-indulgence. It went at the expense of her ambitions—all the while taking a risk with no guarantees of positive results.

This is what I was challenged to understand over time, from sharing my story, aloud, in manuscript, and any other form. I was 24 years old when I was attacked. Life had just started to render itself valid to what I wanted to do, and then in a blink of an eye, I was charged with the responsibility of letting God's people know of His goodness and His miraculous works.

Sure, I could tell the story, but would it convey in such a way that it would save his people. In all honesty, the thought of being a disciple of His works petrified me. I didn't feel worthy of doing so, inadequate. I didn't want to wear a mask of salvation when I had so much work. I wanted to do it for me. My plan, right? Little did I know, "You were chosen for such a time as this," started January 1, 1996.

Going forward, every step of the way, I knew I had a duty to share my story, but still, I wanted to do it on my terms. Unfortunately, during this time, being such an infant in Christ, the pressure from the church community and media set a tone that pushed me into a corner of uncertainty. I never wanted to disappoint God; I knew my survival was all Him; therefore, I didn't want to accept the calling. I was afraid and didn't know how to trust the process. Was I equipped to be a Bondservant of Christ?

Over the years, I learned to conform to share His goodness. Nonetheless, it took a while to realize how organic it really could have been if I would have just believed in myself. Although telling the story was therapeutic, and it left others with their mouths wide open, it would take spiritual confidence to lead others to believe in Him. It is no accident that I am where I am, doing what I'm doing. The Lord has uniquely prepared me to accomplish all endeavors for His Kingdom. Remembering that He has an appointed time for every event in my life. It was never about me, but I was chosen.

He Believes in You

Assignments are given at birth. We were given life so that we could do just that, fulfill our duties according to His will. However, the courage and the stamina that's needed to complete the task are far from within our carnal reach. Belief in self is pure, coupled with a twist of uncertainty.

But the mindset is to know that He would not have given such a task if He didn't think we could handle it. Even during the chaos, whether we choose to see it or not, we are equipped to move purposely through the labyrinth of life. When we learn to trust God in all of who He is, we learn to yield to the expectations that He's set upon us.

My story of triumph is an example of God using all things to perfect His plan for me in my purpose. There have been blessings and hardships along the way, but the method has never changed.

And although God expects His children to live a life of self-denial and humility, He does not want us to give up on ourselves by losing faith and the ability of confidence that He's invested in us.

To keep the faith, I saturate myself in faith-based settings.

This doesn't mean I attend church daily, but It does mean that I incorporate some type of scenery that promotes having faith. Settings as simple as listening to positive music have been known to reassure my faith.

Music is soothing and encourages life's moods. I read inspiring messages, and I dissect them to insert my life's instances. Not only does this help me keep the faith, but it also builds my confidence. Confidence building comes at a time when you reflect on the shoulders of others that you stand. I make it my business to surround myself with people that I admire. People of wisdom who I can assure have endured just as much, if not more.

Yes, I was attacked, but he knew I'd use what he'd invested in me to overcome it. He believed then and still does in me.

Own It

Whether in a mirror or front of a crowd, the message is YOUR message, own it! I can remember when I would first share my story; I'd start with an account of the timeline of events. And although captivating, I'd find myself sounding like a spiritual robot. I knew it was ALL GOD, and none of me that miraculously saved my life, however, I almost forgot it was me that experienced it. God is a God of transparency; He wants to be represented most authentically. So, as the years passed by, I decided that my survival would not be commercialized. And after much prayer, I knew that I was most impactful when I owned my truth of just being myself, allowing my purpose to transcend me.

I can remember a time, shortly after my attack when I was asked to appear on a talk show, the storyline was that of survivorship, and even though I was still somewhat immature in my delivery, I couldn't wait to share. I received a call from the producer who asked me to tell my story, and after doing so, the response was that of a dry sense of fondness. I was a little taken aback until I realized that it had nothing to do with what I thought it should sound like and everything to do with what "that world" was expecting. The producer then went to share that it would be "helpful" if I slow down my words and sadden my tone. I instantly thought to myself this is not an act, and immediately told them that this might not be the show for me to appear on. My story would not be dimmed at the hand of entertainment. Even then, I knew that I'd never want to make my story a story of sadness or shame.

I was reminded that this is your life and your story, the vision that was tailored only for you and nothing or no one, but God can change the narrative. This is when you take the ownership bull by the horns and ride it purposely. The fantastic part about accepting and owning your truth is knowing it's like no one else's, and God did it with you in mind.

A Different Set of Lenses

There comes a time when you start to realize that "your" trauma does have feelings. The most understood sense, initially, in the beginning, is that of fear.

When you learn to evaluate and accept all of that in which it entails, you introduce yourself to the feeling of healing. Not just in the physical realm, but in every aspect of your life. I learned over time that the feeling of being healed allowed me to focus solely on my purpose, ultimately removing the fear that was once prevalent. It's a beautiful feeling.

I also found that it only holds for the person who's been healed. It's usually the person who is at the center of the trauma. It wasn't until recently that I realized that only I could truly understand how to cope with and accept what I'd gone through. Although my support system has always been unwavering, I sometimes felt as if I was the only one my trauma affected. Boy, was I wrong! I knew that those who were there with me during the time of my attack would forever be scarred, what I didn't realize was that just because I felt this sense of healing didn't mean others had. And before I could come to terms with it, I started to equate the same support system with being unattached.

It sometimes left a feeling of loneliness, and the way I dealt with this was to portray the same strength I use to be the "Tamecka" that everyone was expecting.

Sure, I discussed the attack plenty of times, but often felt as if I was the only one in the conversation. Having often heard how others would share the story with strangers, but no one was engaging me. It wasn't until I finally said something about it, that I received a view from a different set of lenses.

I can remember talking with my best friend about it, and she told me, "Hey, you must remember, you'll never be able to see it the way we did, especially when it initially happened.

It was the most horrible thing to witness anyone endure, especially a loved one, and it will forever be etched in our minds, but it's also very liberating when we can share you with others." She went on to say, "Our pride lives within, and we are extremely blessed to have you in our lives, but we will forever be changed by the experience." At that moment, a deep sigh came over me, and I no longer felt lonely, I felt responsible. Not in a negative way, but I knew then that I had a responsibility to those who had been on this journey with me, to make sure I understood their feelings, as not to confuse them with my own.

It's crucial that we feel connected to our loved ones post our traumatic experience. Here are a few ways to ensure this happens:

- Include them in your bad days - there's no room for isolation
- Be sensitive to their lens; they too share in your experience
- Set the tone for the discussion and be open to perception
- Give them your authentic self

My healing would never mirror their healing, and my trauma will never be their trauma, whether I will be at the center or not. Traumatic experiences have their way of making you feel isolated; however, as long as you know that there will always be another set of lenses, you will never be alone.

Divine Timing

In the day and time that we are living, it's so important to connect with kindred spirits. The acts of society are becoming unfathomable, and trauma is more prevalent than ever. Sharing experiences becomes necessary to build a wall of hopefulness. But what about when the stars align, and the "by chances" become more frequent? Let me be the first to say that I don't believe in "by chances". I believe in divine timing.

Divine timing is described as the belief that everything that happens in your life occurs at precisely the right moment. Not that everything that has happened should have, but since it did, it was at the right time.

For this reason, I have no reservations about who I talk to or share my story with. I can remember just recently in preparation of sharing this manuscript along with the many other areas of fulfilling my purpose, I'd scheduled a photoshoot with one of Dallas' most sought out talents in photography. When I first made contact, I was somewhat reluctant to follow through with scheduling because I wasn't sure if I looked the part. However, after a little persistence, I followed through with my appointment. Upon my arrival at the studio, I was pleasantly greeted with the question, "What inspired this photoshoot?"

Well, as God would have it, I asked him if he was a native of Dallas, for the sake of demographics, and I started to share my story. With the first sentence in, I was politely interrupted with the revelation of the photographer completing my next sentence. Not because the story was that familiar or renowned, but it was because he was a first responding witness to it all.

You see, the photographer had been working at the same hospital for a while and was on duty in the ER's radiology department the very night of my attack, and 25 years later, he's still there. He was even able to share with me his account of my emergency room experience, having seen the X-rays of my head before me.

Now, I know we hear that coincidences happen; however, this experience was far from an accident. This was divine. Did I mention, I'd considered calling other photographers, but kept being led back to him? Again, I don't believe in "by chances"; this was always part of God's plan and testimonial.

The photoshoot turned ministry was beyond emotional, and I'm very blessed to have shared this moment with him. I know that it was not "by chance" but by God's design. This meeting was bound before the dirt on the earth, and for this, I am very grateful.

Divinity affords a set of lenses that ultimately help you make sense of things. There's a rational equation that enables you to connect the questionable dots that often present themselves over time. All connections aren't meant to be ah-ha moments. Nevertheless, when they are, it sure does help solve the many unanswered happenings that are presented along the way.

Whether you cross the paths of those you've known for a while or may have just met, when you realize it's part of your purpose, you know having them in your life is part of God's divine plan.

Chapter 9

A Decision and An Action

Post-trauma, "The Will to Live," and "The Will to keep living" sound similar but are governed by two different motives. The will to live is a decision you make when your most profound physical and mental reach fails you, and you're left with nothing but the ability to sponge the desire that you would have it no other way. The will to keep living is an action that takes a daily push from within, that only you can control. Once the decision is made, the action becomes your duty to yourself.

Survivorship, whether it be domestic violence, addiction, disease, the loss of love or a loved one, betrayal, assault, or attempted capital murder, all have a traumatic connotation. And although your trauma will never mirror that of another person, it's essential to know that the will to live and keep living are just as vital to your existence as it was before the trauma was ever presented. Just know that there is no scale or measuring device to use to determine how much time or strength it will take to do both. Once you realize this, you accept the desire and embrace the action like never. You'll get up each day determined to live in it to the fullest. Will life hand you other disparages? Absolutely, but you'll use the same decision and action to keep moving forward. You'll become fueled by the mere fact that you are no doubt an overcomer.

My Story His Glory

If you had told me almost 25 years ago that I'd be the face of inspiration for others near and far, I would have just assumed it to be because of my wittiness. I was blessed with a natural sense of humor, and I love comedy, it's the catalyst that makes me thrive. I would have never thought it would have been at the hands of a near-death experience.

In Hindsight, my childhood, and January 1, 1996, taught me so many things; however, I didn't quite understand how to embrace it right off. Early phases of adjustment brought on the most novice of responses. I often wondered "why me," but when life kept happening, year after year, I was reminded, "why not me." The older I got, the more I knew that I was left here for a purpose. And with that comes a bit of confidence, with no sight of arrogance, when you know that God chooses you for such a feat. You relish in the fact of knowing if He didn't believe you could move on, you would have never been chosen.

There's a saying that "God gives his toughest task to his strongest soldiers." I believe that no matter the rank of the task, we are ALL His soldiers and have a purpose to fulfill and are equipped to be able to do so. Whatever way it was viewed, I knew having survived a brutal stabbing attack, having a pair of scissors embedded six inches in my head (without touching any nerves, vein, or major arteries), along with attempted sexual assault, was nothing short of a Miracle.

We are all Miracles, some with life span shorter or longer than others, and it doesn't take a being notable, famous, or any recognition to determine you are a chosen vessel of God. He knew before the foundation of this earth what your assignment would be for you to carry it out. There will be days of uncertainty; you may not feel like thinking about it at times, but the best advice you can give yourself is to acknowledge it, be authentic, and live through it.

You'll always be faced with questions that you may not ever get the answers to. These are days that you'll spend more time seeking God's face for guidance. Sometimes it won't even make sense.

However, when you know that you've made it past what was designed to defeat you, you find time to revisit the trauma, discuss it with yourself and anyone else who will listen, with hopes of it fueling your next move in your purpose.

Support will be a given. Those that you expect may or may not come through at the right time of vulnerability, yet it would be the instances when you are going about your day to day, that you'll find time to testify to a complete stranger. This will be when you feel most purposeful. The presence of an unmitigated smile or sigh of relief from someone who's story you don't even know, as a response to you sharing yours speaks volumes and adds incentive to your daily plan. It's a Win, Win.

When times of despair creep up, reach deep within your spirit to address the emotions first. Then if you want to cry or have a moment of a tyrant, that's okay, too. Just know that the way this life is set up, you'll have moments that you'll need to address using spiritual and/or professional authentic counsel. The goal here is to grieve OUT not in.

Accepting that you're here to live life to the fullest, becomes therapy. The more life you live, the more you realize that you're not exempt from the circumstances that it comes with. You'll begin to resonate with others and their experiences, and the once unfamiliar world will start to become familiar again.

You are not in this walk alone. And even though the purpose is personal, you'll find your story to sound a little more familiar with each step of the way.

The one forewarning to this is not to allow yourself to build a platform of hopelessness that pushes you to revisit your life before. Days will be different, and most certainly will take more of a push, however, if granted a day more, you give it the respect of gain and not a loss. And remember each day after is a privilege.

Even if the trauma were never to present itself and the usual upheavals of life were just as prevalent, living "Life After" would still apply. These instances are not to define you, but to groom, prepare and build you up. Keep the focus on your goals, remember the most important "whys" of your life, and let this be your reason for reaching them.

Taking time out for yourself should become a habit. Plan a date with you often, as not to get lost in the regression shuffle.

Self-preservation is key.

Self-care is necessary. Surround yourself with as much positivity as you can digest and remain authentic.

These are the nuggets that help remove the sting that comes with "Life After." Remember, you were chosen and trusted. If God is for you, then who would be against you! Through your relationship, you know to Believe in God. However, you must remember HE believes in you. This should bring about a reassurance like never before. This is when you own it, you take it by the horns, and you own it. The trust of God is above that of any other. With each moment, you grow closer to Him, accompanied by a spirit of faith that transcends any doubt that may try to cloud your space and prevent you from fulfilling your purpose post-trauma.

Keep in mind that although your story is yours, it will be viewed by many different lenses. It then becomes your responsibility to nurture, sustain, and foster your vision while at the same time respecting its view from the lenses of others. You are here to share the good news, but it may not feel as good to others as it does to you. That's okay; perception is key and delicate.

As time continues, you'll find yourself in places you would have never thought, with the company of people you wouldn't have ever imagined. Whether in comfort or discomfort, it'll never be by chance. Either way, you should view it as an opportunity to inspire, extend hope, and encourage. You see, this is the way this testimony was set up. I learned to sip from the faucet of transparency and gulp from the cup of humility. It may be My Story, but it's definitely for His Glory.

The Account

My Testimony was tailored for me, just as yours will be tailored for you.

There isn't a day or time to determine when you may have experiences. However, if ever an opportunity is presented to prevent something that may cause one harm, please take it.

"T" was the boyfriend of a schoolmate from years ago in high school.

I knew her well and recognized him as her live-in companion. Their apartment was in the building located next to mine. The night of my attack, they were in the middle of a domestic dispute. She'd left her home for safety that night, and he was challenged with trying to locate her, which only fueled his anger. When I arrived home that night, he'd approach me to use my phone to try to find her. He stated he was locked out of their shared apartment and wanted to see how long it would be before she came home.

I later found out that the part about being locked out wasn't true, and he'd already ransacked the apartment in a fit of rage. My attack occurred from spillover anger, stemming from their dispute.

Once the investigation of my attack was final, and even during court, I learned of several instances they had, concerning domestic violence. She had a pending assault case against him from a prior dispute.

And although my attack was random, it just shows how quickly domestic violence can affect those in and out of your home. You may not always know or see it occur in your own home, but if you ever see something, say something.

If you know of anyone who is experiencing Domestic Violence, please refer to the information below for immediate assistance.

National Domestic Violence Hotline

1 800-799-7233

About Tamecka

Tamecka Grate-Frazier is a native of Dallas, TX, who received her secondary education with the Wilmer Hutchins Independent School District and later earned her bachelor's degree in Business Administration at Northwood University. She's been married for 22 years and is the mother of 3 adult children with one grandson. She's been employed with AT&T for over 20 years and is currently a Consultant in their Human Resource Division. Aside from her career with AT&T, she and her husband are the small business owners of Exclusive Cutz Barbershop. Having fostered this business venture in 2005, as a direct aspiration of her husband, in 2019, Tamecka decided to launch her vision and birth the upcoming release as the newly published author of "Life After." Her debut book tells the story of her survival and purpose, derived from a traumatic experience that changed her life forever in 1996.

Deemed a philanthropist and unmitigated counsel to all humanity, her focus is now to share with others what life looks like after the unthinkable, with hopes that It will reach all of those who have lost hope and can't find their way back to normal. Her main goal is to continue to aspire to inspire, sharing nuggets of her life's experiences to add to the survival guide of others.

Made in the USA
Coppell, TX
19 May 2023

17034167R00067